POCKET THERAPY

for

EMOTIONAL BALANCE

T0299622

MATTHEW MCKAY, PHD

JEFFREY C. WOOD, PSYD

JEFFREY BRANTLEY, MD

New Harbinger Publications, Inc.

PUBLISHER'S NOTE

Distributed in Canada by Raincoast Books

Copyright © 2020 by Matthew McKay, Jeffrey C. Wood,
and Jeffrey Brantley
New Harbinger Publications, Inc.
5674 Shattuck Avenue
Oakland, CA 94609
www.newharbinger.com

Cover design by Sara Christian; Acquired by Elizabeth Hollis Hansen;
Edited by Marisa Solís; Text design by Michele Waters-Kermes and
Amy Shoup

Printed in the United States of America
Library of Congress Cataloging-in-Publication Data on file

Printed in the United States of America

21 20 19

10 9 8 7 6 5 4 3 2 1

First Printing

"The authors of *Pocket Therapy for Emotional Balance* have created a handy, readable guide that brings together simple yet powerful psychological tools for achieving and maintaining emotional well-being. Readers who are willing to seriously and consistently practice as directed will learn effective psychological coping skills, and will likely experience the kind of improved emotional resilience that often results from face-to-face therapy with a skilled dialectical behavior therapy (DBT) provider."

—**Britt H. Rathbone, MSSW, LCSW-C**, expert adolescent therapist, trainer, and coauthor of *What Works with Teens, Dialectical Behavior Therapy for At-Risk Adolescents*, and *Parenting a Teen Who Has Intense Emotions*

"This petite book easily fits in your pocket or purse, and is designed as a quick resource for those struggling with overwhelming distress and emotions. Practical skills are explained in twelve easy-to-read chapters, each with a handy 'explore' section to facilitate bringing skills into everyday life. A great 'go-to' support that you can carry with you at all times."

—**Thomas R. Lynch, PhD, FBPsS**, professor emeritus of clinical psychology in the school of psychology at the University of Southampton, and author of *Radically Open Dialectical Behavior Therapy* and *The Skills Training Manual for Radically Open Dialectical Behavior Therapy*

"*Pocket Therapy for Emotional Balance* is a little gem. McKay, Wood, and Brantley have distilled some of the most potent skills from DBT in terms so clear and concise that anyone, including teenagers, can grasp how to use them. If you struggle with painful or out-of-control emotions, put this little book in your survival kit, or indeed, in your pocket, and remind yourself of how to stay in balance."

—**Cedar R. Koons, LCSW**, DBT consultant and mindfulness teacher, and author of *The Mindfulness Solution for Intense Emotions*

"As a fellow DBT therapist, author, and trainer, I am always on the lookout for simple, practical, and effective ways of making DBT skills usable for the lay reader. In this resource, you will find just that! I was especially impressed by the elegant simplicity with which the authors presented the difficult topics of radical acceptance, wise mind, and self-compassion, all while providing simple exercises to convert theory into immediate practice."

—**Kirby Reutter, PhD**, bilingual clinical psychologist with Department of Homeland Security, and author of *The Dialectical Behavior Therapy Skills Workbook for PTSD*

CONTENTS

CONTENTS

INTRODUCTION

In all of our lives, we have to cope with distress and pain—whether physical, like a beesting or a broken arm, or emotional, like sadness or anger. Both kinds of pain are often unavoidable and unpredictable. The best any of us can do is to use the coping skills we have and hope they work.

But some individuals feel emotional and physical pain more intensely and more frequently than do other people. Their distress comes on more quickly and feels like an overwhelming tidal wave. Often, these situations feel like they'll never end, and the people experiencing them don't know how to cope with the severity of their pain. For the purposes of this book, we'll call this problem *overwhelming emotions.* (But remember, emotional and physical pain often occur together.)

If you struggle with overwhelming emotions, it can seem like the dial is turned to maximum on what you feel. When you get angry or sad or scared, the emotion may show up as a big, powerful wave that sweeps you off your feet.

And when that happens, it can make you afraid to have feelings.

The trouble with that is, the more you try to put a lid on your emotions, the more overwhelming they can get. Trying to stop the feelings doesn't work. Giving in to the feelings causes problems in your relationships and makes life feel out of control.

What does work is a set of tools called *emotion regulation skills.* Those skills are what you'll learn in this guide. Many thousands of people who've struggled with strong emotions have used emotion regulation skills to find what's called *emotional efficacy*—the ability to have real, full emotions (even strong ones) without them running the show. Emotion regulation skills can change lives—including yours.

Emotions Are Information

Emotions are an essential part of being human—they are part of how we survive and function. Basically, emotions are signals within your body that tell you what's happening. When something pleasurable is happening to you, you feel good (joy, pride, satisfaction); when something distressing is happening to you, you feel bad (shame, fear, sadness).

We experience emotions in waves or stages of primary and secondary emotions—and knowing this is key to learning to balance our emotions.

Your initial emotional reaction to what is happening to you is a wave of *primary emotions*. These are strong feelings about what's happening that come on quickly without any thought interference. For example, if you win a contest, you might feel surprised. When someone you care about dies, you feel sad. You don't need to think about the emotion in these cases, it just comes.

Secondary emotions are reactions to your primary emotions. For example, Erik yelled at his sister because she did something that made him feel *angry* (primary emotion). Later he felt *guilty* (secondary emotion) about the things he said when he was so angry with her.

It's possible to respond to a single primary emotion with multiple secondary emotions. For example, Shauna became *anxious* when she was asked to make a future presentation at work. As the day drew closer, she became *depressed* as she thought about how anxious she was getting, and then she started to feel *ashamed* because she couldn't make a simple presentation. Then, the day after the presentation, she felt *guilty* and *ashamed* that she had made such a big deal about it in the first place.

As you might imagine, a primary emotional reaction to a situation can set off a chain reaction of distressing secondary emotions that cause you much more pain than your original emotion does. This is that flood of feelings that swamps you. If you've been dealing with overwhelming emotions for a long time, you might feel frustrated and hopeless about controlling such emotional reactions.

But though it can be difficult to control your primary emotional reaction, you can learn to cope with it. And secondary emotional responses are even easier to learn to control. In this book, you'll build the skills that will let you manage those secondary responses. Later, when you have grown comfortable using these skills, especially the mindfulness skills, you may also gain some control over your primary emotional responses.

Building Emotional Health

Learning how to recognize your emotions and their effect on your life is the first step to controlling your emotional reactions. Very often, people spend their lives paying little attention to how they feel. As a result, there are a lot of important things happening inside them that they know little about.

The same holds true for people struggling with overwhelming emotions, but it occurs in a different way. Very often, people recognize the tidal wave of distressing emotions that overcomes them (such as sadness, anger, guilt, shame, and so on) too late, when there's little they can do about it.

To control overwhelming emotional reactions, it's necessary to slow down the emotional process so that you can examine it. After it's examined, you can make healthier decisions. So in chapter 1, we'll start by learning to identify emotions—the first step in examining them is noticing and naming them.

The skills we'll teach are based in *dialectical behavior therapy (DBT)* which was developed by Marsha Linehan. Drawing on decades of research and clinical practice, DBT teaches critically important skills that can both reduce the size of emotional waves and help you keep your balance when emotions overwhelm you.

DBT isn't complicated; it just takes practice. You'll find you've heard of many of its core concepts, such as mindfulness, acceptance, self-soothing, and relaxation. What DBT does is shape these concepts into learnable skills that you can continue to strengthen and rely on for the rest of your life.

Pocket Therapy for Emotional Balance is written to make learning these skills easy. And, as you might expect, the hard part will be making the commitment to *do* the exercises and put your new skills into practice. To help you, we've built this little book to be a portable, customizable resource.

As you read, we'll guide you to insights about your emotional patterns and help you figure out which tools work for you in various situations. At the end of every chapter is a short section called "Explore," which will help you build a personalized understanding of the chapter's topics. Writing about your insights and experience, whether rough or smooth, will help you find the willingness you'll need to keep at it. You'll need a journal or notebook (or a note app) to do some of this personalized work and to track your progress.

Life can be hard—you already know that. Whatever your experience—regardless of genetics or early pain—you are not stuck or helpless in your struggles with your emotions. If you really do the work in this book, if you really practice the skills as you learn them, your reactions to your feelings will change. This will positively affect the outcome of every conflict and every upset, and can alter the course of your relationships in productive ways.

There is every reason to take courage. All you have to do, just now, is begin.

1

IDENTIFY YOUR
EMOTIONS

Learning to identify your primary emotion in a distressing situation is one thing that will help you cope when the avalanche of secondary emotions overwhelms you. This might sound obvious or easy, but it's usually not—especially when the emotions come on thick and fast. So this first chapter will help you learn to get to the source of an emotional situation, letting you handle it more skillfully.

Let's start by examining a past emotional situation. You'll need to be as honest with yourself as possible. The purpose is to discover what emotions you were feeling (both primary and secondary emotions) and then figure out how those emotions affected your actions and feelings later on.

Here's an example. One evening, Ling came home from work and found her husband drunk on the sofa again. Ling immediately felt angry, so she started screaming at her husband, calling him a "worthless drunk." But he just lay there without arguing or moving. She wanted to hit him, but she didn't.

After a few minutes, Ling started to feel hopeless and ashamed too. She had tried everything to help her husband, but nothing seemed to work. He refused to go to psychotherapy, and he didn't consider himself an alcoholic, so he wouldn't go to a meeting of Alcoholics Anonymous. She didn't feel like she could stay in her marriage if things didn't change, but she also didn't believe in divorce.

Ling went to the bathroom and locked herself in. She thought about killing herself to end the pain she was feeling. Instead, she took out a razor and started cutting herself on her leg, just enough to make herself bleed. That night, still upset, she forgot to set her alarm, and the next day she missed the first few hours of work and got reprimanded by her manager.

Now it's your turn. Pick a situation that you can clearly remember. Then write the questions that follow as headings on blank pages in your journal. Or, if you prefer, visit http://www.newharbinger.com/47674 to download the Recognizing Your Emotions Worksheet. There you can also find a list of common emotions (this can help you name your emotions).

Using Ling's story, let's follow the six-step process that will help you recognize your emotions.

1. *What happened?* Describe the situation that led to your emotions. Write down what happened, when and where, who was involved, and so on. (Ling might write, "I came home and found my husband drunk again. He refuses to get help or to talk about his problem.")

2. *Why do you think that situation happened?* Identify the potential causes of your situation. This step is important: the meaning that you give the event often determines what your emotional reaction is. For example, if you think someone hurt you on purpose, you will react very differently than if you think someone hurt you by accident. (Ling believes that her husband is an alcoholic who hates her and regrets marrying her, which is why he has just given up on his life and why he drinks to hurt her.)

3. *How did the situation make you feel, both emotionally and physically?* Learning to identify your emotions will take practice, but it will be worth the effort. Try

to identify both primary emotions (the ones triggered by the situation) and secondary emotions (the ones triggered by your primary emotions), if you can. If you need help finding words to describe how you feel, see the List of Commonly Felt Emotions (http://www.newharbinger.com/47674). Also, try to identify how you were feeling physically. Emotions and physical sensations, especially muscle tension, are strongly related. (Ling's primary emotion is anger after seeing her husband drunk. Then she feels the secondary emotions of hopelessness and shame. Physically, she notices that all the muscles in her face and arms become very tense, and she feels sick to her stomach.)

4. *What did you want to do as a result of how you felt?* This question identifies your *urges*. Often, when a person is overwhelmed with emotions, he or she has the urge to say or do something that is drastic, painful, or dangerous. However, the person doesn't always do these things; sometimes the urges are just thoughts and impulses. When you start to notice what you *want* to do and compare it with what you *actually* do, the results can be encouraging. If you can control some urges, chances are good that you can control other urges too. (Ling had the urge to do two things that would have been very dangerous, even deadly: hit her husband and kill herself to end her pain. Thankfully, she didn't do

either one, which later gave her
hope that she could control other
urges.)

5. *What did you do and say?* This is
    where you identify *what you actually
    did* as a result of your emotions.
    (Ling locked herself in her
    bathroom and began to mutilate
    herself. She also yelled at her
    husband and called him a
    "worthless drunk.")

6. *How did your emotions and actions
    affect you later?* Identify the
    longer-term consequences of what
    you felt and did. (Ling overslept for
    work the next morning because she
    forgot to set her alarm, and she was
    disciplined by her boss, which put
    her job at risk.)

Say How You're Feeling

To help you recognize your emotions, it helps to say how you're feeling out loud, labeling the emotion. This might sound silly at first, but the act will pinpoint your emotions for you and help you pay extra attention to what you're experiencing. Describing your emotions aloud, especially your overwhelming emotions, can also help deflate distressing feelings. So the more you can *talk* about an emotion, the less urge you might have to *do* something about it.

You don't have to scream how you feel; it might be enough to say your emotion quietly to yourself. Just find what works best for you. Say to yourself, *Right now I feel...* And remember to pay attention to your pleasant and joyful emotions too. The more you're able to recognize those feelings and say them out loud, the more fully you'll be able to enjoy them.

To further reinforce the experience, record your emotions in your journal (or use the Emotional Record worksheet to help you. Visit http://www.newharbinger.com/47674 to download).

About Coping Strategies

People struggling with overwhelming emotions often deal with their pain in very unhealthy, very unsuccessful ways because they don't know what else to do. This is understandable. When a person is in emotional pain, it's hard to be rational and to think of a good solution. Nevertheless, some coping strategies only serve to make our problems worse.

See if any of the following strategies are among your go-tos:

- I spend a great deal of time thinking about past pains, mistakes, and problems.

- I get anxious worrying about possible future pains, mistakes, and problems.

- I isolate myself from other people to avoid distressing situations.

- I make myself feel numb with alcohol or drugs.

- I take my feelings out on other people by getting excessively angry at them or trying to control them.

- I engage in potentially dangerous behaviors, such as cutting, hitting, scratching, picking at, or burning myself, or pulling out my own hair.

- I engage in unsafe sexual activities, such as having sex with strangers or having frequent unprotected sex.

- I avoid dealing with the causes of my problems, such as an abusive or dysfunctional relationship.

- I use food to punish or control myself by eating too much, not eating at all, or by throwing up what I do eat.

- I engage in high-risk activities, like reckless driving or taking dangerous amounts of alcohol and drugs; I may even have contemplated or attempted suicide.

- I avoid pleasant activities, such as social events and exercise, maybe because I don't think that I deserve to feel better.

- I surrender to my pain and resign myself to living a miserable and unfulfilling life.

All of these strategies are paths to even deeper emotional pain, because even the strategies that offer temporary relief will only cause more suffering in the future.

Remember:

Sometimes pain can't be avoided, but many times suffering can.

To avoid long-term suffering, you need to learn the skills that will help you endure and cope with your pain in a new, healthier way.

And you'll get started in the next chapter with a tool called REST, a kind of circuit breaker for coping with pain while avoiding suffering.

Explore

Visit http://www.newharbinger.com/47674 to download The Cost of Self-Destructive Coping Strategies worksheet.

In your journal, write about one or more of the coping strategies listed in this chapter that are your go-tos. Think of times when your coping strategies really got you through a problem, as well as times when your coping strategies came at a cost. (Often, both are true—our strategies both help us and cost us.)

2

TAKE A REST

Now that you've identified some of your own self-destructive and problematic behaviors—and their costs—the first strategy you need to learn is REST, an acronym that reminds you to:

Relax

Evaluate

Set an intention

Take action

Changing any habit is difficult. It requires you to know:

- What actions you want to change

- When you want to change them

- What alternative actions you want to do instead

Equally important, it requires that you *remember* that you want to have a different response in the first place. Often this is the hardest part—especially when you're feeling overwhelmed by your emotions.

So, how do you prepare to make healthier decisions when you're feeling overwhelmed? The first step to changing any problematic or self-destructive behavior—and to *not* act impulsively—is to use the REST strategy: Relax, Evaluate, Set an intention, and Take action.

How to REST

Relax. Stop what you're doing. Take a breath. Step away from the situation for a few seconds to get a different perspective. Don't do what you would normally do; instead, create some "space" between your primary emotional reaction and your urge to act impulsively. Maybe even say out loud, "Stop," "Relax," or "REST." Then take a few slow breaths to help yourself calm down before acting.

Evaluate. What are the facts? Just do a quick evaluation. You *don't* have to figure it all out, and you *don't* have to do an in-depth analysis of why you're feeling the way you do. You don't even have to solve the problem if it's too complicated. Just do your best to get a general sense of what's occurring. Just ask yourself a few simple questions, like: *How do I feel? What's happening? Is anyone in danger?*

Set an intention. An intention is a goal or plan of action. To decide which action you're going to take, ask yourself, *What do I need right now?* Whatever you choose to do right now doesn't have to be the final or best solution to the problem; it simply needs to be something healthy that will help you cope.

Take action. Proceed *mindfully*, which means you move ahead slowly and with awareness of what you're doing. Whatever intention you set, do it now as calmly and effectively as you can.

Again, your first action, taken when you REST, may not be the ultimate solution to the problem at hand. But if you follow these steps, your mindful action is likely to be healthier and more effective than the actions taken if you just reacted impulsively.

Although this four-step process might seem like a lot to do when you're feeling overwhelmed by emotions, with practice these steps can be accomplished in just a few seconds and can become a new habit for you.

Be aware that you might need to use REST more than once in the same situation. If you can't set an effective intention and do an action the first time you REST, start again, taking a few deep, slow breaths between takes.

Even if you just keep "RESTing" for a while—until you feel like the situation is resolved, or until you can effectively get out of the situation—you'll have helped yourself a lot by avoiding impulsive and possibly reckless or damaging behavior.

When to REST?

Usually you'll know there's an opportunity to respond in a different way when you're feeling an intense negative emotion, especially an emotion that makes you want to either a) avoid something, or b) become aggressive with someone. When this happens, REST is a circuit breaker that can give you a choice: either to act impulsively and do what you normally do *or* use one of the coping skills in this book and try a different response.

You may also need to use REST if you're suddenly in pain emotionally, mentally, or physically. This is usually a good indicator that you need to pause, then make a choice.

And last, you might also need to use REST when you notice *the desire* to act impulsively or use one of your usual self-destructive behaviors, *even if you don't know why*.

These three conditions signal a moment of choice: you can either do what you normally do—react impulsively and potentially cause pain for yourself or someone else—or you can Relax, Evaluate, Set an intention, and Take action using a healthier coping skill.

Using REST: Bryan's Story

Bryan frequently started arguments with his wife, Kelly. Usually, he'd end up belittling Kelly, screaming at her that she was "worthless" as a spouse. Afterward, feeling ashamed,

Bryan would rush out to the local bar, where he'd drink too much and spend too much money.

Bryan had just started learning new coping skills, and he knew which ones worked for him. But he often had trouble remembering to use them when he was feeling overwhelmed by anger and depression. He knew he needed to use the REST strategy, so he placed brightly colored sticky notes with the word "REST" on them in several places around his home.

The next time he and Kelly began arguing, he caught sight of one of the sticky notes. Catching his breath, he simply stopped in the middle of what he was yelling, told Kelly he would be back in five minutes, and left the room.

Breathing slowly and deeply in and out, he tried to Relax and to release some of the muscle tension in his body.

Next, he Evaluated the situation, thinking quickly about what was happening. He realized he was arguing with Kelly because she hadn't washed his uniform for work. But he wasn't going to work until the next morning, and he had failed to tell her that he needed it washed in the first place. There was still plenty of time to do it. Bryan recognized that in that moment there was no emergency, but that he was just feeling extremely overwhelmed by his anger.

Bryan felt like leaving home to go to the bar to have a few drinks. Instead, he Set an intention: "I'll stay home, calm down, and not do things that hurt my relationship with Kelly."

Finally, he Took action. Breathing a few more times to calm himself, Bryan went back to where Kelly was. He told her that he recognized he hadn't asked her to wash his uniform, that he was feeling angry, and that he needed to go into the bedroom to calm down. So he went to lie down on the bed, put on some soothing music, and practiced his slow breathing until he felt calm enough to come out and apologize to Kelly.

It was hard for Bryan to remember and then do REST, but once he'd managed to break the circuit on his usual behavior pattern, he successfully made different, more effective—and ultimately healthier—choices.

Practice RESTing

Call to mind a recent situation that caused you to feel emotionally overwhelmed. Do your best to identify what you did impulsively, what self-destructive behavior you engaged in (if any), and how you might have coped with the situation better (maybe not perfectly, but *better*) if you had used the REST strategy.

Answer the following questions on a separate piece of paper or in your journal:

What happened?

How did you feel?

What did you do?

Did you engage in any self-destructive behaviors? If so, what were they?

Using the REST strategy, imagine what could have happened differently.

How could you have **R**elaxed in this situation?

If you had done an **E**valuation, what would you have discovered?

If you had **S**et an intention, what would it have been?

If you had **T**aken action based on that intention, what might have happened?

What might the overall advantages
have been if you had used the REST
strategy?

Making any type of change in your behavior is hard. It's especially hard when you're also challenged by overwhelming emotions at the very moment when you most need to change the behavior! That's why it's important to remind yourself to use REST in conjunction with the skills you'll learn and practice in the rest of this book.

By itself, REST isn't much of a skill. It's more of a strategy that will allow you to incorporate all the coping skills that follow.

Each time you're faced with a challenging situation, feel overwhelmed by your emotions, and need to make a tough choice about what to do, remember to practice REST along with your coping skills. Each time you remind yourself to REST, the more naturally you'll use it in the future.

Explore

In what kinds of situations do you think it will help you to use REST? Think and write a bit about the people, places, and situations that tend to trigger overwhelming emotions in you.

During the next week or so, practice using REST when emotions overwhelm you. Do this at least once, and, when you are able, take out your journal and write about it:

- What was the situation?

- How were you able to **R**elax in this situation? (Breathing, walk around the block, etc.)

- When you **E**valuated, what did you discover?

- When you **S**et an intention, what was it?

- When you **T**ook action in this situation, what was it? Or, if your action is still planned, what will it be?

3

DISTRACT YOURSELF

Our first coping skill is *distraction*. Really. Choosing *when* and *from what* you should distract yourself is a key skill for regulating strong emotions.

Distraction skills are important because:

1. they can temporarily stop you from thinking about your emotional pain and, as a result,

2. they give you time to find an appropriate coping response.

Distraction also buys you time so that your emotions can settle down before you take action to deal with a distressing situation. (It's kind of like the REST strategy in this way.)

Do not confuse distraction with avoidance. When you *avoid* a distressing situation, you're choosing not to deal with it. But when you use skill to *distract* yourself from a distressing situation, you still intend to deal with it in the future, when your emotions have calmed down to a tolerable level.

Do Something Pleasurable

Sometimes doing something that makes you feel good is the best way to distract yourself from painful emotions. Consider going to a museum, taking a bath, doing yoga, or gardening. Remember, you don't have to wait until you feel overwhelmed by painful emotions in order to do a pleasurable activity. In fact, you should try to do something enjoyable every day.

For ideas, visit http://www.newharbinger.com/47674 to find a list of more than one hundred pleasurable activities you can use to distract yourself.

Pay Attention to Someone Else

Another great way to distract yourself from pain is to put your attention on someone else. Here are some examples.

- *Do something for someone else.* Call your friends and ask if they need help doing something, such as a chore, grocery shopping, or housecleaning. Ask your parents, grandparents, or siblings if you can help them with any task.

- *Take your attention off yourself.* Just sit somewhere in public, like a park or mall, and watch other people or walk around among them. Watch what they do. Observe how they dress. Listen to their conversations. Count the number of buttons they're wearing on their shirts.

- *Think of someone you care about.*
  Keep a picture of this person in your phone or in your wallet. This could be someone in your family, a friend, or someone else you admire. Then, when you're feeling distressed, take out the picture and imagine a healing, peaceful conversation with him or her, as if that person were right there with you and could speak to you.

Think of Something Different

The human brain is a wonderful thought-producing machine. Most of the time, this makes our lives much easier. But, unfortunately, we can't fully control what our brain thinks about.

So, instead of trying to force yourself to forget a memory or thought, try to distract your thoughts with other memories or creative images. Here are some examples.

- *Remember happy events from your past.* Try to recall as many details as possible about memories that were pleasant, fun, or exciting. What did you do? Who were you with? What happened?

- *Look at the natural world around you.* Observe the flowers, trees, sky, animals, and landscape as closely as you can. Or if you live in a city without much nature around you, either do your best to observe what you can or close your eyes and imagine a scene you've observed in the past.

- *Imagine yourself as a hero or heroine.* Think about correcting some past or future event in your life. How would you do it? What would people say to you?

- *Imagine yourself getting praise.* Make it from someone whose opinion matters to you. What did you do? What does this person say to you? Why does his or her opinion matter to you?

- *Imagine your wildest fantasy coming true.* What would it be? Who else would be involved? What would you do afterward?

- *Keep a copy of your favorite prayer or saying with you.* Then, when you feel distressed, pull it out and read it to yourself. Imagine the words calming and soothing you. Use imagery (such as a white light coming down from heaven or the universe) that soothes you as you read the words.

Leave the Situation

Sometimes the best thing that you can do is leave. If you're in a very painful situation with someone and you recognize that your emotions are going to overwhelm you and possibly make the situation worse than it is already, then often it's best to just leave.

Remember, if you're already overwhelmed by your emotions, it will be harder for you to think of a healthy resolution to your problem. Maybe it's best to put some distance between you and the situation in order to give yourself time to calm your emotions and think of what to do next. Just walk away if that's the best you can do. It will be better than adding fuel to the emotional fire.

Do Something Useful

Strangely, many people don't schedule enough time to take care of themselves or their living quarters. As a result, tasks and chores go uncompleted. Here, then, is the perfect opportunity to do something to take care of yourself and your environment. The next time you're in a situation in which your emotions become too painful, temporarily distract yourself by doing an activity like washing the dishes, cleaning your room, or mowing the lawn.

Count Something

Counting is a simple skill that can really keep your mind busy and help you focus on something other than your pain. Here are some examples. Identify the ones you're willing to do, and then add any activities that you can think of:

- *Count your breaths.* Sit in a comfortable chair, put one hand on your belly, and take slow, long breaths. Imagine breathing into your stomach instead of your lungs. Feel your belly expand like a balloon with each inhalation. Start counting your breaths. When you inevitably start thinking about whatever it is that's causing you pain, return your focus to counting.

- *Count anything else.* If you're too distracted by your emotions, simply count the sounds that you're hearing. This will take your attention outside of yourself. Or try counting the number of cars that are passing by, the number of sensations that you're feeling, or anything else you can put a number on.

- *Count or subtract by increments of seven.* For example, start with one hundred and subtract seven. Now take that answer and subtract seven more. Keep going. This activity will really distract you from your emotions because it requires extra attention and concentration.

Explore

Put together your distraction plan. First, identify the distraction skills that you're willing to use the next time you're in a situation that's causing you pain and discomfort. (Remember, the first step in your distress tolerance plan should be to use the REST strategy, which will likely include distraction techniques.)

Next, write your chosen distraction techniques on a sticky note to carry around with you in your wallet, or use a note app to record them in your phone. Then, the next time you're in a distressing situation, you can pull out the note or open the app to remind yourself of your distraction plan.

Afterward, it can be helpful to write in your journal about how well your plan and your chosen distraction worked. How might you adjust the plan? This will help you build a repertoire of techniques you can rely on in an emotional crisis.

4

RELAX AND SOOTHE YOURSELF

Now that you've learned some healthy and effective ways to distract yourself when you become overwhelmed by painful emotions, you'll need to learn new ways to help soothe yourself. The activities in this chapter will help you relax, which is the first step in the REST strategy. Then, later in this book, you'll learn specific skills to cope with problematic situations.

Self-Soothing Using Your Senses

Using all five senses, or even just a single one, can be very effective at returning you to the present moment. Each can offer a calming respite from a stressful situation.

Smell: Smell is a very powerful sense that can often trigger memories and make you feel a certain way. Therefore, it's very important that you identify smells that make you feel good, not bad.

Vision: A large portion of our brain is devoted solely to our sense of sight. The things you look at can often have very powerful effects on you, for better or for worse. That's why it's important to find images that have a very soothing impact on you.

Hearing: Certain sounds can soothe us. Listening to gentle music, for example, may be relaxing. Try to identify the sounds that help you relax.

Taste: Our sensations of flavor can trigger memories and feelings, so again, it's important that you find tastes that are pleasing to you.

However, if eating is a problem for you, such as eating too much, bingeing, purging, or restricting what you eat, talk to a professional counselor about getting help for yourself. If the process of eating can make you upset or nervous, use your other senses to calm yourself.

Touch: We often forget about our sense of touch, and yet we're always touching something, such as the clothes we're wearing or the chair we're sitting in. Our skin is our largest organ, and it's completely covered with nerves that carry feelings to our brain.

Below are suggestions for soothing and relaxing using your senses. Identify the ones you're willing to do, and then add any activities you can think of:

- Burn scented candles or incense in your room or house.

- Wear scented oils, perfume, or cologne that makes you feel happy, confident, or sexy.

- Go someplace where the scent is pleasing to you, like a bakery or restaurant.

- Bake food at home that has a pleasing smell, like chocolate chip cookies.

- Buy fresh-cut flowers or seek out flowers in your neighborhood.

- Find a place that has something soothing for you to look at, like a museum.

- Go to the bookstore and find a collection of photographs or paintings that you find relaxing.

- Draw or paint your own picture that's pleasing to you.

- Listen to soothing music. This can be anything that works for you.

- Listen to audiobooks. Many public libraries will let you download or stream audiobooks for free.

- Stream a show, but just listen. Find one that's boring or sedate, not something agitating like the news.

- Open your window and listen to the peaceful sounds outside. Or, if you live in a place without relaxing sounds outside, go visit a place with calming sounds, such as a park.

- Listen to a white-noise machine. *White noise* is a sound that blocks out other distracting sounds. You can buy a machine that makes white noise with circulating air, turn on a fan to block out distracting sounds, or download a white-noise app on your smartphone.

- Enjoy a recording of a meditation or relaxation exercise.

- Listen to the sound of rushing or trickling water. Maybe your local park has a water feature or the nearby mall has a fountain.

- Enjoy your favorite meal, whatever it is. Eat it slowly so you can take pleasure in the way it tastes.

- Carry nuts, gum, or a nutrition bar with you to eat when you're feeling upset.

- Eat a soothing food that makes you feel good.

- Drink something soothing, such as tea. Practice drinking it slowly so you can enjoy the way it tastes.

- Suck on an ice cube or an ice pop, especially if you're feeling warm, and enjoy the taste as it melts in your mouth.

- Buy a piece of juicy fresh fruit and then eat it slowly.

- Carry something soft or velvety in your pocket to touch when you need to, like a piece of cloth.

- Take a warm or cold shower and enjoy the feeling of the water falling on your skin.

- Take a warm bubble bath or a bath with scented oils and enjoy the soothing sensations on your skin.

- Get a massage.

- Massage yourself. Sometimes just rubbing your own sore muscles is very pleasing.

- Play with your pet.

- Wear your most comfortable clothes, like your favorite worn-in T-shirt, baggy sweat suit, or old jeans.

Take a Time-Out

Time-outs aren't just for kids. We all need to relax in order to refresh our bodies, minds, and spirits. Yet many people don't take time out for themselves because they feel like they'd be disappointing someone else, like their boss, spouse, family, or friends.

Many people ignore their own needs because they feel guilty or selfish about doing anything for themselves. But how long can you continue to take care of someone else without taking care of yourself? You need to take care of yourself, and that doesn't mean you're selfish.

Here are some simple ideas you can use to take time out for yourself. Identify the ones you're willing to do.

- Treat yourself as kindly as you treat other people. Do one nice thing for yourself that you've been putting off, such as making yourself a delicious meal or treating yourself to a massage.

- Take time to devote to yourself, even if it's just a few hours during the week. This might include a five-minute meditation before work or writing in a gratitude journal before going to bed.

- If you're feeling really brave, take a half day off from work. Go someplace beautiful, like a park, the ocean, a lake, the mountains, a museum, or even someplace like a shopping center.

- Take time to do things for your own well-being, like getting a haircut, taking an exercise class, making a doctor's appointment, and so on.

Explore

Now that you've read the suggestions to help you relax and soothe yourself using your five senses, construct a list of techniques you're willing to use. For ideas, review the activities that you identified. Be specific about what you're going to do. Make a list of ideas to try at home and another list of ideas to use when you're away from home. Keep these lists in convenient places that are easy to remember, like in an app on your smartphone.

As with your distraction techniques, it can be helpful to write in your journal about how well your relaxation plan worked. How might you adjust the plan? Again, this will help you build a repertoire of techniques you can rely on to get you through an emotional crisis.

5

USE DEEP
RELAXATION

The skills in this chapter can quickly reduce the intensity of your overwhelming emotions. Two of the many purposes of your nervous system are *survival* and *relaxation*. In survival mode, the nervous system turns on the fight, flight, or freeze response in your body that is necessary for survival, like a faster heart rate and increased muscle tension. In contrast, the relaxation response causes an opposite set of reactions to occur—such as decreased heart rate and reduced muscle tension—which helps you rest and feel at ease.

The physiological coping skills that you're about to learn in this chapter turn on the relaxation response by triggering biological responses in the human body.

Cue-Controlled Relaxation

Cue-controlled relaxation is a quick and easy technique that will help you reduce your stress level and muscle tension. A *cue* is a trigger or command that helps you relax. In this case, your cue will be a word, like "relax" or "peace." The goal of this technique is to train your body to release muscle tension when you think about your cue word.

Initially, you'll need the help of the guided instructions to help you release muscle tension in different parts of your body. But after you've been practicing this technique for a few weeks, you'll be able to relax your whole body at one time simply by taking a few slow breaths and thinking about your cue word. With practice, this can become a speedy way to help you relax. Before you begin, choose a cue word that will help you relax.

To begin this exercise, you'll need to find a comfortable chair to sit in. Later, after you've practiced this exercise for a few weeks, you'll be able to do it wherever you are, even if you're standing. You'll also be able to do it more quickly. But to begin, choose a comfortable place to sit in a room where you won't be disturbed. Make sure you'll be free from distractions.

Read the following directions before you begin. If you feel comfortable remembering them, close your eyes and begin the relaxation exercise. Or, if you prefer, record the instructions on your smartphone. Then close your eyes and listen to the guided relaxation technique that you created.

To begin, sit in a comfortable chair with your feet flat on the floor and your hands resting comfortably, either on the arms of the chair or in your lap. Close your eyes.

Take a slow, long breath in through your nose. Feel your belly expand like a balloon as you breathe in. Hold it for five seconds: 1, 2, 3, 4, 5.

Then release it slowly through your mouth. Feel your belly collapse like a balloon losing its air.

Again, take a slow, long breath in through your nose and feel your stomach expand. Hold it for five seconds: 1, 2, 3, 4, 5. Then exhale slowly through your mouth.

One more time: Take a slow, long breath in through your nose and feel your stomach expand. Hold it for five seconds: 1, 2, 3, 4, 5. Then exhale slowly through your mouth.

Now begin to take slow, long breaths without holding them, and continue to breathe smoothly for the rest of this exercise.

Now, with your eyes still closed, imagine that a white beam of light shines down from the sky like a bright laser and lands on the very top of your head. Notice how warm and soothing the light makes you feel. This could be a light from God, the universe, or whatever power makes you feel comfortable.

As you continue to breathe smoothly, taking slow, long breaths, noticing how the light makes you feel more and more relaxed as it continues to shine on the top of your head.

Now, slowly, the warm, white light begins to spread over the top of your head like soothing water. And as it does, the light begins to loosen any muscle tension that you're feeling on the top of your head.

Slowly, the light begins to slide down your body, and, as it moves across your forehead, all the muscle tension there is released. Then the white light continues down past your ears, the back of your head, your eyes, nose, mouth, and chin, and it continues to release any tension you're holding there. Notice how pleasantly warm your forehead feels.

Now, slowly, imagine that the light begins to move down your neck and over your shoulders, releasing any muscle tension. Then the light slowly proceeds down both of your arms and the front and back of your torso. Feel the muscles in your upper and lower back release. Notice the soothing sensation of the white light as it moves across your chest and stomach. Feel the muscles in your arms release as the light moves down to your forearms and then across both sides of your hands to your fingertips.

Now notice the light moving down through your pelvis and buttocks, and feel the tension being released. Again, feel the light move like soothing water across your upper and lower legs until it spreads across both the upper and lower surfaces of your feet. Feel all of the tension leaving the muscles of your body as the white light makes your body feel warm and relaxed.

Continue to notice how peaceful and calm you feel as you continue to take slow, long, smooth breaths. Observe how your stomach continues to expand as you inhale, and feel it deflate as you exhale.

Now, as you continue breathing, silently think to yourself breathe in *as you inhale, and then silently think your cue word as you exhale.* [If your cue word is something other than "relax," use that word in the following instructions.] *Slowly inhale and think:* breathe in. *Slowly exhale and think:* relax. *As you do, notice your entire body feeling relaxed at the same time. Feel all the muscle tension in your body being released as you focus on your cue word.*

Again, inhale and think: breathe in. *Exhale and think:* relax. *Notice your entire body releasing any muscle tension. Again, inhale...* breathe in. *Exhale...* relax. *Feel all the tension in your body releasing.*

Continue breathing and thinking these words at your own pace for several minutes. With each breath, notice how relaxed your entire body feels. When your mind begins to wander, return your focus to the words "breathe in" and "relax."

Practice the cue-controlled relaxation technique twice a day and record how long it takes you to feel relaxed. With daily practice, this technique should help you relax more quickly each time. Again, remember that the ultimate goal of this technique is to train your entire body to relax simply when you think of your cue word, such as "relax." This will only come with regular practice.

Progressive Muscle Relaxation

Progressive muscle relaxation is a technique of systematically tightening and relaxing specific muscle groups in order to soothe anxiety and help you relax. This technique was created by physician Edmund Jacobson in the early twentieth century, and the results of his research were eventually published in his book *Progressive Relaxation* in 1929. With regular practice, Dr. Jacobson discovered that this muscle relaxation technique not only relieves immediate distress, but it can also prevent future distress because the muscles of the body cannot be both relaxed and tense at the same time.

Most people are not aware of the muscle tension that they hold in their bodies. The next time you're in a group of people, notice how many people struggle with muscle tension in their bodies. Look for the hunched shoulders, the poor posture, the tight jaws, the clenched fists, and the grimaces on so many faces.

Unfortunately, many of us have become so used to carrying tension in our bodies that we just accept it as being "normal." But whether it's normal or not, it can still be corrected in most cases.

Progressive muscle relaxation focuses on helping you recognize the difference between a tight, tense feeling in your muscles versus a loose, relaxed feeling. In order to help you recognize the sensations more easily, progressive muscle relaxation focuses on tensing and releasing small groups of muscles, one at a time. By intentionally shifting your muscles from tense to relaxed, you learn to recognize the difference between the two states. And in the future, when you do hold tension in those muscles, you'll be able to more easily spot the tension and release it.

Here's how to do it.

Starting with one of your hands, methodically tense and release groups of muscles. For example, begin with your left hand, wrist, and forearm; then your left upper arm and shoulder; then go to your forehead; eyes and cheeks; mouth and jaw; neck; right hand, wrist, and forearm; and so on.

As you move through each muscle group, you'll contract the muscles for approximately five seconds and then quickly release the muscle tension. It's important that you release the tension as quickly as you can so that you're better able to distinguish the relaxed feeling. Then take fifteen to thirty seconds to notice the feeling of your muscles releasing and relaxing.

Then tighten and release the same group of muscles again, and continue to notice the difference between the tight feeling and the relaxed feeling. In general, tighten and release each group of muscles at least twice, but if you need additional focus on a particular group of muscles to help them release, you can tighten and release them up to five times.

You can practice progressive muscle relaxation while you are either seated or lying down, and, with practice, you can even tense and release some muscles on the go while you are walking and standing.

Pick a verbal cue to use while you are relaxing. By repeatedly pairing a verbal cue with the act of relaxing your muscles, you can eventually train your muscles to relax simply by using your word, as you learned with cue-controlled relaxation.

Before beginning progressive muscle relaxation, consider your physical limitations, if any, and proceed with extra caution if you currently have any back, neck, joint, or shoulder pain. Even if your health is not a concern, proceed with caution as you tense muscles in your back, neck, and feet. Never tighten these areas so much that they cause you pain.

Explore

When you practice a new skill or technique regularly for a period of time, you not only get better at it and more comfortable with it, but you're also making it into a tool you can reach for when you need it. You can also start to notice a range of results. Sometimes the practice will be just what you need at the moment; sometimes it will feel kind of pointless.

During the next week, practice one of the relaxation techniques in this chapter every day. Afterward, write down a few things you noticed about the practice and its effect on you. The next week, practice and write about the other one. Which one would you like to be able to turn to in a moment of stress? (Or maybe you turn to both!) Keep practicing that one, scheduling it every day *and* pulling it out when you find you need it.

6

TRY RADICAL
ACCEPTANCE

Increasing your ability to tolerate distress
starts with a change in your attitude. You're
going to need something called *radical acceptance,* which is a new way of looking at your
life.

Often, when a person is in pain, his or
her first reaction is to get angry or upset, or to
blame someone for causing the pain in the
first place. But, unfortunately, no matter who
you blame for your distress, your pain still
exists and you continue to suffer. In fact, in
some cases, the angrier you get, the worse
your pain will feel.

Getting angry or upset over a situation
also stops you from seeing what is really happening. Have you ever heard the expression
"being blinded by rage"? This often happens
to people with overwhelming emotions.
Criticizing yourself or others all the time or
being overly judgmental of a situation is like
wearing dark sunglasses indoors. By doing

this, you're missing the details and not seeing everything as it really is. By getting angry and thinking that a situation should never have happened, you're missing the point that it *did* happen and that you have to deal with it.

Being overly critical about a situation prevents you from taking steps to change that situation. You can't change the past. And if you spend your time fighting the past—wishfully thinking that your anger will change the outcome of an event that has already happened—you'll become paralyzed and helpless. Then nothing will improve.

So what else can you do?

The other option, which radical acceptance suggests, is to acknowledge your present situation, whatever it is, without judging the events or criticizing yourself. Try to recognize that your present situation exists because of a long chain of events that began far in the past.

For example, some time ago, you (or someone else) thought you needed help for the emotional pain you were experiencing. So, a few days later, you went to the bookstore (or went online) and bought this book. Then today, you thought about reading this chapter, and eventually you sat down, opened the book, and began reading. Now, you are up to the words you see here.

Denying this chain of events does nothing to change what has already happened. Trying to fight this moment or saying that it shouldn't be like this only leads to more suffering for you. Radical acceptance means looking at yourself and the situation, and seeing them as they really are.

Keep in mind that radical acceptance does *not* mean that you condone or agree with bad behavior in others. But it does mean that you stop trying to change what's happened by getting angry and blaming the situation.

For example, if you're in an abusive relationship and you need to get out, then get out. Don't waste your time and continue to suffer by blaming yourself or the other person. That won't help you. Refocus your attention on what you can do now. This will allow you to think more clearly and figure out a better way to cope with your suffering.

Radical Acceptance Coping Statements

To help you begin using radical acceptance, it's often worthwhile to use a coping statement to remind yourself. Below are a few examples. Identify the statements that you'd be willing to use to remind yourself to accept the present moment and the chain of events that created it. In the next exercise, you'll begin using the statements that you chose.

"This is the way it has to be."

"All the events have led up to now."

"I can't change what's already happened."

"It's no use fighting the past."

"Fighting the past only blinds me to my present."

"The present is the only moment I have control over."

"It's a waste of time to fight what's already occurred."

"The present moment is perfect, even if I don't like what's happening."

"This moment is exactly as it should be, given what's happened before it."

"This moment is the result of a
million other decisions."

Radical acceptance means that you accept
something completely, without judging it. For
example, radically accepting the present
moment means that you don't fight it, get
angry at it, or try to change it into something
that it's not.

To radically accept the present moment,
you must acknowledge that the present
moment is what it is due to a long chain of
events and decisions made by you and other
people *in the past*. The present moment never
spontaneously leaps into existence without
being caused by events that have already
taken place. Imagine that each moment of
your life is connected like a line of dominoes
that knock each other down.

But remember, radically accepting something doesn't mean that you give up and

simply accept every bad situation that happens to you. Some situations in life are unjust, such as when someone abuses or assaults you. But for other situations in life, you share at least some responsibility. There's a balance between what you created and what others have created.

However, many people struggling with overwhelming emotions often feel as if life just "happens" to them, not recognizing their own role in creating a situation. As a result, their first reaction is to get angry. In fact, one client once told us that anger was her "default emotion," meaning that when she was just being herself, she was angry. Her excessive hostility caused her to hurt herself—by drinking heavily, cutting herself, and constantly berating herself—and it also led to her hurting the people she cared about by constantly arguing with them.

In contrast, radically accepting the present moment opens up the opportunity for you to recognize the role that you have played in creating your current situation. And, as a result, it also creates an opportunity to respond to that situation in a new way that's less painful for yourself and others.

In many ways, radical acceptance is like the Serenity Prayer, which says: "Grant me the serenity to accept the things I cannot change, the courage to change the things I can, and the wisdom to know the difference."

To practice radical acceptance during an upsetting event, it helps to pause and ask yourself some grounding questions. You can also practice when you're not in a painful situation. Let's try it right now.

Think of a distressing situation that you experienced recently. Then answer these questions that will help you radically accept the situation in a new way. You can download a worksheet for this exercise at http://www.newharbinger.com/47674.

1. What happened in this distressing situation?

2. What past events happened that led up to this situation?

3. What role did I play in creating this situation?

4. What roles did other people play in creating this situation?

5. What *do* I have control of in this situation?

6. What *don't* I have control of in this situation?

7. What was my response to this situation?

8. How did my response affect my own thoughts and feelings?

9. How did my response affect the thoughts and feelings of other people?

10. How could I have changed my response to this situation so that it led to less suffering for myself and others?

11. How could the situation have occurred differently if I had decided to radically accept the situation?

It's very important to remember that radical acceptance also applies to accepting yourself. In this case, radical acceptance means embracing who you are without judging or criticizing yourself. Or, to put it another way, radically accepting yourself means loving yourself just the way you are, with all of your goodness and all of your faults.

Finding the goodness inside of yourself might be a difficult challenge, especially if you're struggling with overwhelming emotions. Many people with this problem often think of themselves as being defective, bad, or unlovable. As a result, they overlook their good qualities and add more pain to their lives. This is why radically accepting yourself is so extremely important.

Explore

Use the coping statements you learned in this chapter to practice radically accepting situations without being judgmental or critical. Here are some ways to practice:

- Read a controversial story in the newspaper without being judgmental about what has occurred.

- The next time you get caught in heavy traffic, wait without being critical.

- Watch the world news on television without being critical of what's happening.

- Listen to a news story or a political commentary on the radio without being judgmental.

In your journal, write about the experience.

Can you think of some other ways to practice this way of letting go and letting the world be what it is?

7

LIVE IN THE PRESENT

Time travel is possible. We all do it occasionally, but some people do it more often than others. People who time travel spend a large portion of each day thinking about all the things they should've done yesterday, all the things that went wrong in the past, and all the things they're supposed to do tomorrow. As a result, that's where they live, in the past or in the future. They rarely pay attention to what's happening to them right now, so they miss living in the present moment—the only true moment in which anyone can really live.

Often, we don't pay attention to what's happening to us. We don't pay attention to what people are saying to us or to the things that we read. We don't even pay attention to who's around us while we're walking. And to make it even more problematic, we often try to do more than one thing—like driving, eating, texting, and talking on the phone—at the same time. As a result, we miss a lot of what life has to offer, and we often make easy situations more difficult.

But even worse, not living in the present moment can also make life more painful. For example, maybe you anticipate that the person with whom you're talking is going to say something insulting, which makes you feel angry—even though the person hasn't even said anything yet!

Or maybe just thinking about past events makes you feel physically or emotionally upset, which then interferes with whatever you're trying to do in that moment. Obviously, both types of time traveling can make any event unnecessarily painful.

Try the following exercises to help you live in the moment and tolerate distressing events more skillfully.

"Where Are You Now?"

The next time you're in a distressing situation, ask yourself the following questions:

- Where am I right now?

- Am I time traveling in the future, worrying about something that might happen, or planning something that might happen?

- Am I time traveling in the past, reviewing mistakes, reliving bad experiences, or thinking about how my life could have been under different circumstances?

- Or am I in the present, really paying attention to what I'm doing, thinking, and feeling?

If you're not in the present moment, refocus your attention on what's happening to you now by using the following steps:

- Notice what you're thinking about and recognize if you're time traveling. Bring your focus back to the present moment.

- Notice how you're breathing. Take slow, long breaths to help you refocus on the present.

- Notice how your body feels and observe any tension or pain you might be experiencing. Recognize how your thoughts might be contributing to how you're feeling. Use cue-controlled relaxation to release any tension.

- Notice any painful emotions you might be feeling as a result of time traveling, and use one of the distress tolerance skills to help you relieve any immediate pain.

Listening to Now

Here's another exercise to help you refocus on the present moment. Dedicate at least five minutes to help yourself refocus. Set a timer so you can really sink into the moment. Read the following directions before you begin. If you feel comfortable remembering them, close your eyes and begin. Or, if you prefer, record the instructions on your smartphone. Then close your eyes and listen to the guided relaxation technique that you created.

Sit in a comfortable chair. Turn off any distractions, like your phone, radio, computer, and television, and close your eyes.

Take slow, long breaths in through your nose and out through your mouth. Feel your stomach expand like a balloon each time you breathe in, and feel it deflate each time you exhale.

Now, as you continue to breathe, simply listen. Listen to any sounds you hear outside your home, inside your home, and inside your own body. Count each sound that you hear.

When you get distracted, return your focus to listening. Maybe you hear cars, people, or airplanes outside. Perhaps you hear a clock ticking or a fan blowing inside. Or maybe you hear the sound of your own heart beating inside your body. Actively and carefully listen to your environment and count as many sounds as you can.

A variation of this listening exercise can help you stay focused on the present moment while you're in conversation with another person: If you notice that your attention is beginning to wander and you start thinking about your past or future, focus your attention on something that the other person is wearing, like a button on his or her shirt, a hat he or she is wearing, or the collar of the shirt. Note to yourself what color the item is and what it looks like. Sometimes this can snap you out of your time traveling. Now, continue to listen, and if your mind begins to wander again, repeat the refocusing steps and try to keep listening to what the other person is saying.

Focus on a Single Minute

This exercise will help you focus more fully on the present moment. It's simple to do, but it often has an amazing effect. Its purpose is to help you become more mindful of your own sense of time. For this exercise, you'll need a watch with a second hand or a stopwatch app on your smartphone.

To begin this exercise, find a comfortable place to sit in a room where you won't be disturbed for a few minutes, and turn off any distracting sounds. Begin timing yourself with your watch or smartphone. Then, without counting the seconds or looking at the watch, simply sit wherever you are.

When you think that one minute has passed, check the watch again or stop the timer. Note how much time really has passed.

Did you allow less than a full minute to pass? If so, how long was it: a few seconds, twenty seconds, forty seconds? If it wasn't a full minute, consider how this affects you. Are you always in a rush to do things because you don't think you have enough time? If so, what does the result of this exercise mean for you?

Or did you allow more than a minute to pass? If so, how long was it: one and a half minutes, two minutes? If so, consider how this affects you. Are you frequently late for appointments because you think that you have more time than you really do? If so, what does the result of this exercise mean for you?

Whatever your results, one of the purposes of learning mindfulness skills is to help you develop a more accurate awareness of all your moment-to-moment experiences, including your perception of time.

Explore

Try each of the exercises in this chapter at least twice. Then write in your journal about the experiences with the help of these writing prompts:

- Did "Where Are You Now?" help you manage a distressing situation? If you had trouble remembering the steps in the moment, consider simply asking, *Where am I now?* and then taking and releasing two deep, slow breaths, then repeating the question and the breaths.

- When you tried the other exercises, did you experience moments of being in the now? What did being in the moment feel like in your mind and body?

8

USE MINDFULNESS

Mindfulness, also known as meditation, is a valuable skill that has been taught for thousands of years in many of the world's religions. So what exactly is mindfulness? For the purposes of this book:

> *Mindfulness is the ability to be aware of*
> *your thoughts, emotions, physical sensations,*
> *and actions—in the present moment—*
> *without judging or criticizing yourself,*
> *others, or your experience.*

Have you ever heard the expressions "be in the moment" or "be here now"? These are both different ways of saying "be mindful of what's happening to you and around you." But this isn't always an easy task. At any moment in time, you might be thinking, feeling, sensing, and doing many different things. The truth is, no one is 100 percent mindful all the time. But the more mindful you learn to be, the more control you will gain over your life.

But remember, time never stands still, and each second of your life is different. Because of this, it's important that you learn to be aware "in each present moment."

For example, by the time you finish reading this sentence, the moment that you started reading it is gone and your present moment is now different. In fact, *you* are now different. The cells in your body are constantly dying and being replaced, so physically you're different. Equally important, your thoughts, feelings, sensations, and actions are never exactly the same in every situation, so they're different too. For these reasons, it's important that you learn to be mindful of how your experience changes in each individual moment of your life.

In order to be fully aware of your experiences in the present moment, it's necessary that you do so without criticizing yourself, your situation, or other people. In dialectical behavior therapy, this is called *radical acceptance*. As described in chapter 6, radical acceptance means tolerating something without judging it or trying to change it. This is important, because if you're judging yourself, your experience, or someone else in the present moment, then you're not really paying attention to what's happening in that moment.

For example, many people spend a lot of time worrying about mistakes they've made in the past or worrying about mistakes that they might make in the future. But while they're doing this, their focus is no longer on what's happening to them *now*; their thoughts are somewhere else. As a result, they live in a painful past or future, and life feels very difficult.

So to review, mindfulness is the ability to be aware of your thoughts, emotions, physical sensations, and actions—in the present moment —without judging or criticizing yourself, others, or your experience.

Mindful Awareness of Emotions

Mindful awareness of your emotions starts with focusing on your breathing—just noticing the air moving in through your nose and out through your mouth, filling and emptying your lungs. Then, after four or five slow, long breaths, shift your attention to how you feel emotionally in the present moment. Start by simply noticing whether you feel good or bad. Is your basic internal sense that you are happy or not happy?

Then see if you can observe your emotion more closely. What word best describes the feeling? Consult the list of emotions (available at http://www.newharbinger.com/47674)

if you're having trouble finding the most accurate description.

Keep watching the feeling and, while you do, continue describing to yourself what you observe. Notice the nuances of the feeling or perhaps the threads of other emotions woven into it. For example, sometimes sadness has veins of anxiety or even anger. Sometimes shame is intertwined with loss or resentment. Also notice the strength of your emotion and check to see how it changes while you watch it.

If you have difficulty finding an emotion that you're feeling in the present moment, you can still do this exercise by locating a feeling that you had in the recent past.

However you choose to observe an emotion, once the emotion is clearly recognized, stay with it. Keep describing to yourself the changes in quality, intensity, or type of emotion you're feeling. Ideally, you should observe the feeling until it has significantly changed—in quality or strength—and you have some sense of the wave effect of your emotion.

While watching your feeling, you'll also notice thoughts, sensations, and other distractions that try to pull your attention away. This is normal. Just do your best to bring your focus back to your emotion whenever your attention wanders. Just stay with it until you've watched long enough to observe your emotion grow, change, and diminish.

As you learn to mindfully observe a feeling, two important realizations can emerge. One is the awareness that all feelings have a natural life span. If you keep watching your emotions, they will peak and gradually subside.

The second awareness is that the mere act of describing your feelings can give you a degree of control over them. Describing your emotions often has the effect of building a container around them, which keeps them from overwhelming you.

Let's now move slowly through the steps of mindfully watching your emotions. First, read all of the directions to familiarize yourself with the experience. If you think you might be more comfortable hearing the instructions while practicing this technique, use your smartphone to record the directions in a slow, even voice. If you record the directions, pause between each paragraph so that you can leave time to fully experience the process later.

Take a long, slow breath and notice the feeling of the air moving in through your nose, going down the back of your throat, and into your lungs. Take another breath and watch what happens in your body as you inhale and let go. Keep breathing and

*watching. Keep noticing the sensations in your
body as you breathe.* [Pause for one minute.]

*Now turn your attention to what you feel
emotionally. Look inside and find the emotion you
are experiencing right now. Or find an emotion
that you felt recently. Notice whether the emotion
is a pleasant or an unpleasant feeling. Just keep
your attention on the feeling until you have a
sense of it.* [Pause for one minute.]

*Now look for words to describe the emotion. For
example, is it elation, contentment, or excitement?
Is it sadness, anxiety, shame, or loss? Whatever it
is, keep watching and describing the emotion in
your mind. Notice any change in the feeling and
describe what's different. If any distractions or
thoughts come to mind, do your best to let them
go without getting stuck on them. Notice whether
your feeling is intensifying or diminishing, and
describe what that's like.* [Pause for one minute.]

Keep observing your emotion and letting go of distractions. Keep looking for words to describe the slightest change in the quality or intensity of your feeling. If other emotions begin to weave in, continue to describe them. If your emotion changes into an altogether new emotion, just keep observing it and finding the words to describe it. [Pause for one minute.]

Thoughts, physical sensations, and other distractions will try to grab your attention. Notice them, let them go, and return your focus to your emotion. Stay with it. Continue observing it. Keep going until you've observed your emotion change or diminish.

Explore

Choose one or more mindfulness skills to practice daily during at least the next two weeks. Which will you practice? When, where, and for how long? Making a plan, including scheduling a time and setting a reminder, will make it much more likely you'll succeed at getting a mindfulness practice going.

Once you've been practicing your mindfulness skills for a couple of weeks, return to the Focus on a Single Minute exercise in the preceding chapter. Has your perception of time changed, if at all?

9

PRACTICE MINDFUL
BREATHING

Very often, when you're distracted by your thoughts and other stimuli, one of the easiest and most effective things you can do is to focus your attention on the rising and falling of your breath. This type of awareness also causes you to take slower, longer breaths, which can help you relax.

In order to breathe mindfully, you need to pay attention to three parts of the experience. First, you must count your breaths. This will help you focus your attention, and it will also help you calm your mind when you're distracted by thoughts.

Second, you need to focus on the physical experience of breathing. This is accomplished by observing the rising and falling of your chest and stomach as you inhale and exhale.

And third, you need to be aware of any distracting thoughts that arise while you're breathing. Then you need to let the thoughts go without getting stuck on them. Letting go of the distracting thoughts will allow you to refocus your attention on your breathing and help you further calm yourself.

The following mindful breathing exercise will help you learn to separate your thoughts from your emotions and physical sensations. First, read the directions all the way through to familiarize yourself with the experience. If you think you might be more comfortable hearing the instructions while practicing this technique, use your smartphone to record the directions in a slow, even voice.

When you first start this practice, try it for three to five minutes. Then, as you get more accustomed to using this technique, try it for ten or fifteen minutes. This is such a simple and powerful skill that, ideally, you should practice it every day.

First, find a comfortable place to sit in a room where you won't be disturbed for as long as you've set your timer. Turn off any distracting sounds. If you feel comfortable closing your eyes, do so to help you relax.

To begin, take a few slow, long breaths and relax. Place one hand on your stomach. Now slowly breathe in through your nose, and then slowly exhale through your mouth. Feel your stomach rise and fall as you breathe.

Imagine your belly filling up with air like a balloon as you breathe in, and then feel it effortlessly deflate as you breathe out. Feel the breath moving in across your nostrils, and then feel your breath blowing out across your lips, as if you're blowing out candles.

As you breathe, notice the sensations in your body. Feel your belly move as you activate the diaphragm muscle and allow your lungs to fill up with air. Notice the weight of your body resting on whatever you're sitting on. With each breath, notice how your body feels more and more relaxed.

Now, as you continue to breathe, begin counting your breaths each time you exhale. You can count either silently to yourself or aloud. Count each exhalation until you reach 4 and then begin counting at 1 again.

To start, breathe in slowly through your nose, and then exhale slowly through your mouth. Count 1. Again, breathe in slowly through your nose and slowly out through your mouth. Count 2. Repeat, breathing in slowly through your nose, and then slowly exhale. Count 3. Last time—breathe in through your nose and out through your mouth. Count 4. Now begin counting at 1 again.

This time, though, as you continue to count, occasionally shift your focus to how you're breathing. Notice the rising and falling of your chest and abdomen as you inhale and exhale. Again, feel the breath moving in through your nose and slowly out through your mouth.

If you want to, place your other hand on your abdomen and feel your breath rise and fall. Continue counting as you take slow, long breaths. Feel your belly expand like a balloon as you breathe in, and then feel it deflate as you breathe out. Continue to shift your focus back and forth between counting and the physical experience of breathing.

Now, begin to notice any thoughts or other distractions that remove your focus from your breathing. These distractions might be memories, sounds, physical sensations, or emotions. When your mind begins to wander and you catch yourself thinking of something else, return your focus to counting your breath. Or return your focus to the physical sensation of breathing.

Try not to criticize yourself for getting distracted. Just keep taking slow, long breaths into your belly, in and out. Imagine filling up your belly with air like a balloon. Feel it rising with each inhalation and falling with each exhalation. Keep counting each breath and, with each exhalation, feel your body relaxing more and more deeply.

Keep breathing until your alarm goes off. Continue counting your breaths, noticing the physical sensation of your breathing and letting go of any distracting thoughts or other stimuli. Then, when your alarm goes off, slowly open your eyes and return your focus to the room.

Slow Breathing

You've already learned how to use mindful breathing as a skill to help you stay focused in the present moment. But regulating the overall rate at which you breathe can also help you relax when you're experiencing distress and anxiety.

The slow-breathing technique that you'll learn next is a distress tolerance technique that you can practice for three to five minutes each day. But don't worry, you're *not* expected to breathe this slowly throughout an entire day. Rather, think of this as another distress tolerance skill that you should practice in a calm atmosphere before you really need it in a time of heightened emotion. With enough practice, you will then be able to use this coping technique when presented with a very stressful situation.

If at any point during this exercise you feel dizzy, light-headed, or faint, or notice tingling in your lips or fingertips, stop the exercise and return your breathing rate to normal. Feelings like this typically indicate that you're hyperventilating, meaning you're breathing too quickly. Try the technique again later, breathing more slowly, once you feel stable.

First, read the directions all the way through to familiarize yourself with the experience. If you think you might be more comfortable hearing the instructions while practicing this technique, use your smartphone to record the directions in a slow, even voice, then play it back when you're ready to practice.

―――――――――

To begin, find a comfortable place to sit in a room where you won't be disturbed for as long as you've set your timer. Turn off any distracting sounds. Take a few slow, long breaths and relax.

Place one hand on your stomach. Now slowly breathe in through your nose, and then slowly exhale through your mouth. Feel your stomach rise and fall as you breathe. Imagine your belly filling up with air like a balloon as you breathe in, and then feel it effortlessly deflate as you breathe out. Feel the breath moving in across your nostrils, and then feel your breath blowing out across your lips, as if you're blowing out birthday candles.

Now, as you continue to breathe, begin counting the length of both your inhalations and exhalations. Count silently to yourself as you watch your timer. As you slowly breathe in, think: In, 2. Then as you start to breathe out, think: Out, 2, 3, 4. Then start the pattern again: In, 2. Out, 2, 3, 4. In, 2. Out, 2, 3, 4.

Continue to silently pace your breaths, doing your best to take slow, steady breaths. Slow, steady breaths. Try not to breathe too quickly. Remember, you do not have to fill up your entire lung capacity. Rather, think of slow breaths moving in and out of your belly, gently filling it up with air like a balloon.

In, 2. Out, 2, 3, 4. In, 2. Out, 2, 3, 4. In, 2. Out, 2, 3, 4.

When your mind gets distracted, or when you lose count of your breaths, just gently return your focus to your breath moving in and out of your belly, or refocus on your counting.

In, 2. Out, 2, 3, 4. In, 2. Out, 2, 3, 4. In, 2. Out, 2, 3, 4.

Keep breathing until your timer goes off, and then slowly return your focus to the room.

Explore

Once you sense that you have a good ability to do slow breathing or mindful breathing, set an intention to do a field test. That is, use either technique in a stressful situation in the coming week—one in which you have used REST.

Afterward, when you have a few moments, write about the experience in your journal. Do you think that using a mindful breathing skill along with REST helped you cope with the situation more effectively than you might otherwise have done?

10

USE WISE-MIND MEDITATION

Wise *mind* is the ability to make healthy decisions about your life. The term "wise mind" has been used previously in Buddhist mindfulness practices. It describes a person's ability to simultaneously recognize two things: first, that he or she is suffering (from ailments, overwhelming emotions, or the results of unhealthy actions), and second, that he or she also wants to be healthy and has the potential to change.

The original developer of DBT, Marsha Linehan, has acknowledged that Zen Buddhist practices greatly influenced the development of dialectical behavior therapy, so it is not surprising that DBT also recognizes that a person needs to both accept his or her pain while simultaneously engaging in actions that help alleviate that pain.

And one of the primary tools to achieving this goal in DBT is also to use wise mind, the ability to make decisions based on both your rational thoughts and your emotions. This might sound easy to do, but let's consider the traps that many people often fall into.

Emotion mind occurs when you make judgments or decisions based solely on how you feel. But keep in mind that emotions themselves are not bad or problematic. We all need emotions to live healthy lives. The problems associated with emotion mind develop when your emotions *control* your life. This trap is especially dangerous for people with overwhelming emotions, because emotion mind distorts your thoughts and judgments, and then these distortions make it hard to formulate healthy decisions about your life.

The balancing counterpart to emotion mind is *reasonable mind*. Reasonable mind is the part of your decision-making process that analyzes the facts of a situation, thinks clearly about what is happening, considers the details, and then makes rational decisions.

Obviously, rational thinking helps us solve problems and make decisions every day. But again, as with emotions, too much rational thinking can also be a problem. We all know the story of the very intelligent person who didn't know how to express his or her emotions and, as a result, lived a very lonely life. So here, too, a balance is needed in order to live a fulfilling, healthy life. But for people with overwhelming emotions, balancing feelings and rational thought is often hard to do.

The solution is to use wise mind to make healthy decisions about your life. Wise mind results from using both emotion mind and reasonable mind together. Wise mind is a balance between feelings and rational thoughts.

Wise Mind and Intuition

According to dialectical behavior therapy, wise mind is similar to intuition. Often, both intuition and wise mind are described as "feelings" that come from "the gut," or the stomach area. The exercise that follows will help you get more in touch with your gut feelings, both physically and mentally. This exercise will help you locate the center of wise mind in your body. This is the spot from which many people report knowing what to do and making sensible, wise-mind decisions about their lives.

Interestingly, this phenomenon of gut feelings might be supported by scientific evidence. Researchers have discovered that a vast web of nerves covers your digestive system. This web of nerves is second in complexity only to the human brain, so some researchers have referred to this area as the *enteric brain*, meaning the brain in the stomach.

Wise-Mind Meditation

When you begin using this technique, set a timer for three to five minutes and practice this exercise until the alarm goes off. Then, as you get more accustomed to using this technique, you can set the alarm for longer periods of time, like ten or fifteen minutes. If you feel more comfortable being guided through the instructions, use your smartphone to record the directions in a slow, even voice so that you can listen to them while practicing this technique.

To begin, find a comfortable place to sit in a room where you won't be disturbed for as long as you've set your timer. Turn off any distracting sounds. If you feel comfortable closing your eyes, do so to help you relax.

Now, locate the bottom of your sternum on your rib cage. You can do this by touching the bone at the center of your chest and then following it down toward your abdomen until the bone ends. Now place one hand on your abdomen between the bottom of your sternum and your belly button. This is the center of wise mind.

Take a few slow, long breaths and relax. Now slowly breathe in through your nose, and then slowly exhale through your mouth. Feel your abdomen rise and fall as you breathe. Imagine your belly filling up with air like a balloon as you breathe in, and then feel it deflate as you breathe out.

Feel the breath moving in across your nostrils and then feel your breath blowing out across your lips, as if you're blowing out candles. As you breathe, notice any sensations in your body. Feel your lungs fill up with air. Notice the weight of your body as it rests on the seat on which you're sitting. With each breath, notice how your body feels, and allow your body to become more and more relaxed.

Now, as you continue to breathe, let your attention focus on the spot underneath your hand. Let your attention focus on the center of wise mind. Continue to take slow, long breaths. If you have any distracting thoughts, just allow those thoughts to leave you without fighting them and without getting stuck on them. Continue to breathe and focus on the center of wise mind. Feel your hand resting on your stomach.

As you focus your attention on your center of wise mind, notice what appears. If you've had any troubling thoughts, problems, or decisions that you have to make in your life, think about them for a few seconds.

Then, ask your center of wise mind what you should do about these problems or decisions. Ask your inner intuitive self for guidance, and then notice what thoughts or solutions arise out of your center of wise mind. Don't judge whatever answers you receive. Just note them to yourself and keep breathing. Continue to focus your attention on your center of wise mind. If no thoughts or answers come to your questions, just continue breathing.

Now, continue to notice your breath rising and falling. Keep breathing and returning your focus to the center of wise mind until the timer goes off. Then, when you've finished, slowly open your eyes and return your focus to the room.

Making Wise-Mind Decisions

Now that you've had practice locating your wise-mind center, you can check in with that area of your body before you make decisions. This can help you determine whether a decision is a good one. To do this, simply think about the action you are about to take and focus your attention on your center of wise mind. Then consider what your wise mind tells you. Does your decision feel like a good one? If so, then maybe you should do it. If it doesn't feel like a good decision, then maybe you should consider some other options.

Learning to make reliably good decisions about your life is a process that evolves as long as you are alive, and there is no single way to do this. Checking in with your center of wise mind is simply *one* way that works for some people.

However, some words of caution are needed here. When you first use wise mind to make decisions about your life, it will probably be difficult to tell the difference between an intuitive gut feeling and a decision made the old way with emotion mind. The difference can be determined in three ways:

1. *When you made your decision, were you being mindful of both your emotions and the facts of the situation?* In other words, did you make the decision based on both emotion mind and reasonable mind? If you haven't considered the facts of the situation and are being controlled by your emotions, you're not using wise mind. Sometimes we need to let our emotions settle and cool off before we can make a good decision. If you've recently been

involved in a very emotional situation, either good or bad, give yourself enough time for your hot emotions to cool down so that you can use reasonable mind.

2. *Did the decision feel right to you?* Before you make a decision, check in with your center of wise mind and notice how it feels. If you check in with your center of wise mind and you feel nervous, maybe the decision you're about to make isn't a good one or a safe one. However, maybe you feel nervous because you're excited about doing something new, which can be a good thing. Sometimes it's hard to tell the difference, and that's why

using reasonable mind to make your decision is also important. Later, when you have more experience making healthy decisions for your life, it will be easier to tell the difference between a good nervous feeling and a bad nervous feeling.

3. *Have you examined the results of your decision?* If your decision leads to beneficial results for your life, chances are you used wise mind to make that decision. When you start using wise mind, keep track of your decisions and the results in order to determine whether you're *really* using wise mind. Remember, wise mind should help you make healthy decisions about your life.

Explore

In your journal, use the wise-mind criteria to assess whether a decision you've made recently was a wise-mind decision:

- Describe the ways your decision making did or didn't balance both facts and emotions.

- Write about the ways it did or didn't feel right.

- Consider whether the results were, by and large, beneficial.

Visit http://www.newharbinger.com/47674 to download How to Make Wise-Mind Decisions.

11

INCREASE YOUR
POSITIVE EMOTIONS

In recent years, health psychologists have begun to look more deeply at "positive" emotions and attitudes, and their role in promoting health. The rich tradition of positive mental health inquiry builds on the work of psychologists Gordon Allport and Abraham Maslow in the 1960s and continues strongly today. It is motivated in large part by an interest in developing an expanded vision of human capacity and potential. Of particular interest on this theme is that expanded human potential has been one of the primary goals of meditation training since ancient times.

Contemporary health psychologists and researchers Shauna L. Shapiro and Gary E. R. Schwartz have written about the positive aspects of meditation. They point out that mindfulness is about how one pays attention. Shapiro and Schwartz name five "heart" qualities to incorporate into a mindfulness meditation practice to increase positive emotions: gratitude, gentleness, generosity, empathy, and loving-kindness.

Loving-kindness, in particular, can be a powerful aid to your mindfulness practice. All you need to do is to admit and allow feelings of kindness and compassion into your way of paying attention mindfully. Resting in kindness this way, *with compassion and affection embedded in your attention*, can protect you from the deep habits of judging and criticism, and support you in being truly nonjudgmental.

Loving-Kindness

The following is a brief meditation practice to cultivate loving-kindness for yourself and for others. Practice it whenever and for as long as you like. Try it as a lead-in to any of your formal mindfulness practices. If you feel more comfortable being guided by the instructions, use your smartphone to record the directions in a slow, even voice so that you can listen to them while practicing this technique.

Take a comfortable position. Bring your focus mindfully to your breath or body for a few breaths. Open and soften as much as feels safe to you as you allow yourself to connect with your natural inner feelings of kindness and compassion for others. [Pause for a minute.]

Now shift your attention to yourself. It could be a sense of your whole self or some part that needs care and attention, such as a physical injury or the site of an illness or a feeling of emotional pain.

Imagine speaking gently and quietly to yourself, as a mother speaks to her frightened or injured child. Use a phrase like "May I be safe and protected" or "May I be happy" or "May I be healthy and well" or "May I live with ease," or make up one of your own. Let the phrase you pick be something anyone would want (safety, ease, joy, and so on). Pick one that works for you. It can be a single phrase. Then put all your heart into it each time you speak to yourself. Let kindness and compassion come through you. [Pause for one minute.]

Practice by repeating your phrase to yourself silently as if singing a lullaby to a baby. Practice for as long as you like. It may help to practice for just a few minutes at a time at first and later build up to a longer practice.

When you like, you can shift your attention and focus to a friend or someone you know who is troubled. You can also focus on groups of people, such as "all my friends" or "all my brothers and sisters." [Pause for one minute.]

You can also experiment with difficult people in your life. Try sending them kindness and your wish that they might be happy, and watch your inner response. In doing loving-kindness for a difficult person, you are *not* allowing them to abuse or hurt you but are making an attempt to see that they, too, are human beings who seek happiness. This can change your relationship to the situation and release you from any resentment you may be holding.

Please note that in doing a loving-kindness meditation, you are likely to experience many different feelings! Some may even be disturbing, such as sadness, grief, or anger. If this happens, you have *not* made a mistake. It is common for deeply held feelings to be released as one practices loving-kindness. This release is actually a kind of healing in itself. Just pay attention to all of your feelings, honoring each one, and continue your practice.

Compassion for Yourself

To *have compassion* for someone means to recognize that the person is in pain and needs
help. Similarly, when we *show compassion* for
others, we treat them kindly and don't judge
them for their situation or feelings—regardless of whose fault it is. Yet, for so many of us
human beings, it's often easier to help and
forgive others—even complete strangers—
rather than to be kind to ourselves. So why is
it so much easier to be compassionate toward
others and more difficult to be compassionate toward yourself?

Maybe you think that other people are
more deserving of help and respect than
you are.

Maybe you think you've done so many
things wrong that no one can forgive you
and you don't deserve to be treated
compassionately.

Maybe you're afraid of acknowledging that you are in pain because you're afraid of being overwhelmed by it.

Maybe you think that forgiving yourself is the same as excusing your behavior and avoiding consequences.

Or maybe no one has ever treated you compassionately in the past, so you think there's something wrong with you.

In fact, none of these statements is true. Imagine if one of your most beloved friends or family members came to you and said, "I don't deserve compassion because I _____ [fill in one of the statements above]." You would likely disagree with him or her and try to convince him or her otherwise. Similarly, now is the time to start practicing compassion for yourself and to acknowledge that you deserve kindness and help, just like everyone else.

Regardless of the beliefs that are keeping you stuck, being compassionate with yourself is one of the most important skills you can learn in this book. You need self-compassion in order to make any lasting improvements in your life. Every type of self-help work—whether it's getting help from a therapist or using this book—starts with self-compassion. Self-compassion is a belief that you are *deserving* of kindness, forgiveness, and help—just like everyone else!

The truth is that we all make mistakes in our lives, and some of those mistakes unfortunately hurt ourselves or others. However, it doesn't help to keep punishing yourself for the mistakes you've made; that only makes the situation worse.

In many ways, self-compassion requires the use of radical acceptance. Remember, radical acceptance is the skill of letting go of judgments and acknowledging what is actually occurring in your life due to a long chain of events. Self-compassion requires the same thing.

It's time to acknowledge that you are the person you are, with a history of unchangeable events, *and* you still deserve peace, safety, health, and happiness. Starting right now, you can radically accept who you are with all of your past mistakes *and* start making healthier, values-based decisions in your life. Because you deserve happiness and forgiveness, just like everybody else!

There's also one more important reason why you deserve compassion: because you have experienced great pain in your life. You've had losses. You've likely experienced rejection or abandonment at some point. You've faced physical pain and illness. And you've likely experienced disappointment when something you desperately wanted didn't happen.

It's likely that you also suffered similar hurts and losses in childhood, and memories of those experiences may still cast shadows on your life. Plus, you have likely suffered with feelings of shame, sadness, and fear—and these same painful feelings continue to show up in your life now.

You deserve compassion because you've had to face your share of pain and struggle. Wouldn't you feel compassion for another human being who's suffered like this—even a stranger? So, shouldn't you extend the same amount of compassion to yourself?

Use the following meditation to develop and reinforce your sense of self-compassion. Practice it regularly and throughout the day whenever you have an opportunity to be kind to yourself, such as forgiving yourself when you make a mistake, making healthy snack choices, and practicing patience with your decisions (or indecisions!).

Self-Compassion Meditation

Use this self-compassion meditation to develop and strengthen your ability to show kindness and acceptance toward yourself. To begin, use mindful breathing to help yourself relax and focus. As with the other meditations in this book, read the directions all the way through first, to familiarize yourself with the experience. If you think you might be more comfortable hearing the instructions while practicing this technique, use your smartphone to record the directions in a slow, even voice.

Find a comfortable place to sit in a room where you won't be disturbed. Turn off any distracting sounds. If you feel comfortable closing your eyes, do so to help you relax.

To begin, take a few slow, long breaths, and relax.
Place one hand on your stomach. Now slowly
breathe in through your nose and then slowly
exhale through your mouth. Feel your stomach
rise and fall as you breathe. Imagine your belly
filling up with air like a balloon as you breathe in,
and then feel it deflate as you breathe out.

Feel the breath moving in across your nostrils, and
then feel your breath blowing out across your lips.
As you breathe, notice the sensations in your
body. Feel your lungs fill up with air. Notice the
weight of your body resting on whatever you're
sitting on. With each breath, notice how your body
feels more and more relaxed. [Pause for thirty
seconds.]

Now, as you continue to breathe, begin counting
your breaths each time you exhale. You can count
either silently to yourself or aloud. Count each
exhalation until you reach 4, and then begin
counting at 1 again.

To begin, breathe in slowly through your nose, and then exhale slowly through your mouth. Count 1. Again, breathe in slowly through your nose and slowly out through your mouth. Count 2. Repeat, breathing in slowly through your nose, and then slowly exhale. Count 3. Last time—breathe in through your nose and out through your mouth. Count 4. Now begin counting at 1 again. [Pause for thirty seconds.]

Now bring your awareness inside your own body, noting the world of sensation there at this very moment. You live in this body—allow yourself to be aware of your breath, your life force. As you hold that awareness, slowly repeat the following phrases (either silently or aloud) on each exhalation of your breath:

"May I be peaceful."

"May I be safe."

"May I be healthy."

"May I be happy and free from suffering."

Now repeat the phrases two or three more times, allowing their meaning to deepen each time. Allow yourself to feel and accept your own sense of compassion. [Repeat the phrases two or three more times if you are recording the instructions.]

Finally, when you are done, take a few additional slow breaths, rest quietly, and savor your own sense of goodwill and compassion.

Explore

In your journal, answer the following questions:

- What are the thoughts and feelings that come up when you read that you deserve compassion and that you are allowed and encouraged to give it to yourself?

- When you practice feeling loving-kindness for others, or compassion for yourself, using the structured meditations, what happens?

- Do you think you can be willing to keep practicing these skills and find out what happens?

12

COPE ON THE SPOT

Often, people with overwhelming emotions go through similar distressing situations over and over again. So, in some ways, these situations are predictable. In this chapter, you'll identify what those past situations are (and continue to be), how you cope with them, and what the unhealthy consequences have been. Then you'll identify what new coping strategies you can use in the future if you experience similar situations. You'll also discover what the healthier consequences might be as a result of using those new strategies.

Use Self-Encouraging Thoughts

There are many distressing times in life when we all need to hear some encouraging words to keep us motivated or to help us endure the pain that we're experiencing. But there are many distressing times like these when you are simply alone—and you need to encourage yourself to stay strong. Often, this can be done with self-encouraging *coping thoughts*.

Coping thoughts are reminders of how strong you've been in the past when you survived distressing situations, and they're also reminders of encouraging words that have given you strength. Coping thoughts are especially helpful when you first notice that you're feeling agitated, nervous, angry, or upset. If you can recognize your distress early on, you'll have a better chance of using one of these thoughts to help soothe yourself. Maybe there are even situations in your life that occur on a regular basis when you can predict that one of these coping thoughts might be useful.

Here is a list of some coping thoughts that many people have found to be helpful. Make a note of the ones that are helpful to you, and also create your own.

"This situation won't last forever."

"I've already been through many other painful experiences, and I've survived."

"This too shall pass."

"My feelings make me uncomfortable right now, but I can accept them."

"I can be anxious and still deal with the situation."

"I'm strong enough to handle what's happening to me right now."

"This is an opportunity for me to learn how to cope with my fears."

"I can ride this out and not let it get to me."

"I can take all the time I need right now to let go and relax."

"I've survived other situations like this before, and I'll survive this one too."

"My _____ [anxiety, fear, sadness, etc.] won't kill me. It just doesn't feel good right now."

"These are just my feelings, and eventually they'll go away."

"It's okay to feel _____ [anxiety, fear, sadness, etc.] sometimes."

"My thoughts don't control my life—I do."

"I can think different thoughts if I want to."

"I'm not in danger right now."

"So what?"

"This situation sucks, but it's only temporary."

"I'm strong and I can deal with this."

Coping thoughts can help you tolerate distressing situations by giving you strength and motivation to endure those experiences.

Now that you know about coping thoughts, you can begin using them immediately. Write your five favorite coping thoughts on a sticky note and put them in your wallet or hang them in a conspicuous place where you can see them every day, like on your refrigerator or bathroom mirror. Or, if you want to have them with you all the time, put them in a note app in your smartphone. The more you see your coping thoughts, the more quickly they will become part of your automatic thought process.

Record stressful situations in which you can use your coping thoughts to give you strength, or download the Coping Thoughts Worksheet at http://www.newharbinger.com /47674 and keep it with you so that you can record the experience as soon as it happens. Recording the experience quickly might be awkward or inconvenient for you, but doing it this way will help you remember to use your self-encouraging coping thoughts more often.

Coping Alone or with Others

It's very likely that you'll need to use different coping strategies when you're alone versus when you're with someone else. For example, when you're alone and feel overwhelmed, it might be most effective to use cue-controlled relaxation or mindful breathing techniques to soothe yourself. But these techniques might be awkward or impossible to use when you're with someone else. So, you'll need to be prepared with other skills for situations with others, such as taking a time-out or using a coping thought.

Explore

Pick four distressing situations from the past and examine how you coped with them. Identify the unhealthy coping strategies you used and the consequences to you and anyone else who was involved. Then record which new skills from this book could have been used to cope with those situations in a healthier way. Finally, consider what healthier consequences may happen if you use your new coping strategies.

EMOTIONAL BALANCE TOOL KIT

When emotions are overwhelming you, your best first aid tool is REST (see chapter 2). REST gives you a chance to use your coping skills. Use this space to list your most effective coping skills (including their page numbers in this guidebook), and turn to this page when you need to REST, cope, and reset.

_____

_____

_____

_____

_____

_____

_____

_____

_____

_____

_____

_____

_____

_____

_____

_____

_____

_____

_____

_____

_____

_____

_____

_____

_____

_____

_____

_____

_____

_____

_____

_____

_____

_____

_____

_____

_____

_____

_____

_____

_____

_____

_____

_____

Matthew McKay, PhD, is a professor at the Wright Institute in Berkeley, CA. He has authored and coauthored numerous books, including *The Dialectical Behavior Therapy Skills Workbook*, *The Relaxation and Stress Reduction Workbook*, *Self-Esteem*, *Thoughts and Feelings*, *When Anger Hurts*, and *ACT on Life Not on Anger*. McKay received his PhD in clinical psychology from the California School of Professional Psychology, and specializes in the cognitive behavioral treatment of anxiety and depression.

Jeffrey C. Wood, PsyD, lives and works in Las Vegas, NV. He specializes in brief therapy treatments for depression, anxiety, and trauma. He also provides coaching for spiritual development, communication skills development, and life-skills coaching. He is coauthor of *The New Happiness*, *The Dialectical Behavior Therapy Skills Workbook*, *The Dialectical Behavior Therapy Diary*, *The Cognitive Behavioral Therapy Workbook for Personality Disorders*, and *Getting Help*.

Jeffrey Brantley, MD, is a consulting associate in the Duke University department of psychiatry, and founder and director of the Mindfulness Based Stress Reduction (MBSR) program at Duke Integrative Medicine. He has represented the Duke MBSR program in numerous radio, television, and print interviews. He is author of *Calming Your Anxious Mind*, and coauthor of *Five Good Minutes*.

More Pocket Therapy—
On-the-Go Guides
for Immediate Relief

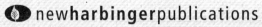

Real change *is* possible

For more than forty-five years, New Harbinger has published proven-effective self-help books and pioneering workbooks to help readers of all ages and backgrounds improve mental health and well-being, and achieve lasting personal growth. In addition, our spirituality books offer profound guidance for deepening awareness and cultivating healing, self-discovery, and fulfillment.

Founded by psychologist Matthew McKay and Patrick Fanning, New Harbinger is proud to be an independent, employee-owned company. Our books reflect our core values of integrity, innovation, commitment, sustainability, compassion, and trust. Written by leaders in the field and recommended by therapists worldwide, New Harbinger books are practical, accessible, and provide real tools for real change.

 newharbingerpublications